THE SCIENCE BEHIND
BATMAN'S
TOOLS

by
Agnieszka Biskup

BATMAN created by
Bob Kane with Bill Finger

CAPSTONE PRESS
a capstone imprint

Published by Capstone Press in 2016
A Capstone Imprint
1710 Roe Crest Drive
North Mankato, Minnesota 56003
www.mycapstone.com

STAR36690

Library of Congress Cataloging-in-Publication Data
Names: Biskup, Agnieszka, author.
Title: The science behind Batman's tools / by Agnieszka Biskup.
Description: North Mankato, Minnesota : Capstone Press, 2016. | 2016 |
   Series: DC super heroes. Science behind Batman | Audience: Ages 7-9. | Audience: K to grade 3. | Includes
   bibliographical references and index.
Identifiers: LCCN 2016002660| ISBN 9781515720386 (library binding) | ISBN 9781515720423 (paperback) | ISBN
   9781515720461 (ebook (pdf))
Subjects: LCSH: Batman (Fictitious character)—Juvenile literature. | Crime prevention—Technological
innovations—Juvenile literature. | Inventions—Juvenile literature. | Technology—Juvenile literature.
Classification: LCC HV8073 .B554 2016 | DDC 600—dc23
LC record available at http://lccn.loc.gov/2016002660

Summary: Explores the real-world science and engineering connections to the tools in Batman's Utility Belt.

Editorial Credits
Christopher Harbo, editor; Hilary Wacholz, designer; Wanda Winch, media researcher;
Tori Abraham, production specialist

Artwork by Luciano Vecchio and Ethen Beavers

Photo Credits
Alamy: louise murray, 20, National Geographic Creative/Gregory A. Harlin, 13 (top), WaterFrame, 21; Getty
Images: AFP/Kazhuiro Nogi, 9; Shutterstock: digitalreflections, 13 (bottom), farres, 8, Gavran333, 7, Joe White,
14 (t), PinkBlue, 17 (t), Sergio Schnitzler, 12, Tooykrub, 15; Thinkstock: manxman, 14 (b); U.S. Army photo by
Markus Rauchenberger, 11; U.S. Marine Corps photo by Cpl. David Hernandez, 18; U.S. Navy photo by John
Narewski, 19, Mass Communications Specialist Seaman Martin Carey, 16

Printed in China.
007727

TABLE OF CONTENTS

INTRODUCTION
ULTIMATE TOOL KIT

Many super heroes use special tools to fight crime. Wonder Woman has her Golden Lasso of Truth. Green Lantern uses a power ring. But Batman carries a whole tool kit. His Utility Belt is packed with amazing gear. Best of all, much of it exists in the real world.

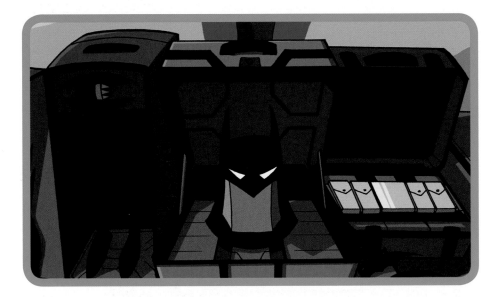

Green Lantern's power ring harnesses his willpower to do almost anything.

Batman's Utility Belt carries all of his tools, gadgets, and weapons.

Wonder Woman's Golden Lasso of Truth forces anyone held by it to tell the truth.

CHAPTER 1

BATARANGS AND GRAPNELS

Batman carries several
types of Batarangs.

Some Batarangs return like **boomerangs**. A boomerang's wings tip sideways as it spins through the air. This **motion** causes it to curve in flight. Thrown correctly, a boomerang will return to the thrower.

A boomerang is held correctly when its curve points toward the thrower.

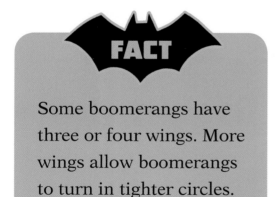

FACT

Some boomerangs have three or four wings. More wings allow boomerangs to turn in tighter circles.

boomerang—a curved stick that spins and turns in flight; some boomerangs are made to return to the thrower

motion—moving or being moved

The Dark Knight often uses Batarangs to smash windows and lights. Japanese **ninjas** once used *shuriken* in a similar way. These throwing weapons were usually thin, star-shaped metal plates. With a flick of the wrist, ninjas sent shuriken spinning through the air.

FACT

Some shuriken were straight, spikelike blades. They were thrown overhand like a baseball pitch.

Star-shaped shuriken had between three and eight razor-sharp points.

Modern-day ninja Jinichi Kawakami displays a collection of traditional Japanese weapons.

ninja—someone who is highly trained in Japanese martial arts and stealth

Batman uses a **grapnel** gun to help him climb buildings. It **launches** a hook and rope onto a roof.

In our world, soldiers use grappling hooks too. The U.S. Army even has a tool for launching them. The T-PLS can fire a grappling hook and rope 120 feet (37 meters) into the air.

A soldier practices throwing a grappling hook during training.

grapnel—a hook with four or five prongs

launch—to send something into the air

CHAPTER 2
BOLAS AND BOMBS

When villains run, the Caped Crusader uses bolas to trip them up. A bola has several weights connected by cords. People have hunted with bolas for thousands of years. The weapons helped catch animals by wrapping around their legs and wings.

Some traditional bolas used leather sacks filled with stones for weights.

Ancient hunters used bolas to catch prey.

FACT

A modern lawn game is played by throwing two-ball bolas onto a plastic ladder.

Batman uses smoke bombs to cover his escapes. Some real smoke bombs are fireworks. These hollow clay or cardboard containers are packed with smoke-making chemicals. When lit, the chemicals burn to release thick clouds of smoke.

Smoke bombs come in different sizes and shapes and can release all sorts of colors.

FACT

Soldiers often use smoke **grenades** as signals.
They can release red, orange, green, blue,
purple, black, or white smoke.

grenade—a small bomb that can be thrown or launched

The Dark Knight also distracts enemies with flash grenades. Soldiers and police officers use flashbang grenades to confuse enemies. Flashbangs release a blinding light and an ear-splitting bang. The blast can cause short-term blindness and hearing loss.

A soldier throws a flashbang during a training exercise.

Soldiers and police officers use flashbangs during drug raids and hostage situations.

FACT

A flashbang's blast is louder than a jet engine. It can affect the **fluid** in the inner ear and cause enemies to lose their sense of balance.

fluid—a liquid or gas substance that flows

17

CHAPTER 3
PERISCOPES AND REBREATHERS

Batman's periscope helps him see around walls in secret. Periscopes use mirrors to **reflect** light around corners. Light coming into the periscope bounces off one mirror and travels to a second mirror. This mirror shows the user a picture from around the corner.

A Marine using a hand-held periscope.

photonics masts

Some submarines use photonics masts instead of periscopes. These masts use sensors and cameras to show images on a display panel inside the submarine.

reflect—to bounce off an object

For underwater missions, the Caped Crusader relies on his rebreather. These devices allow divers to rebreathe their own air. Rebreathers remove harmful gases the diver breathes out. Leftover **oxygen** is then breathed in again.

A military diver uses a rebreather to move through the water.

oxygen—a colorless gas in the air that people and animals need to live

scuba gear

rebreather

A diver using a rebreather doesn't release bubbles like a diver using scuba gear.

From Batarangs to rebreathers, Batman's Utility Belt carries everything he needs. Many real-world tools are as amazing as those used by the Dark Knight himself.

GLOSSARY

boomerang (BOO-muh-rang)—a curved stick that spins and turns in flight; some boomerangs are made to return to the thrower

fluid (FLOO-id)—a liquid or gas substance that flows

grapnel (GRAP-nuhl)—a hook with four or five prongs

grenade (gruh-NAYD)—a small bomb that can be thrown or launched

launch (LAWNCH)—to send something into the air

motion (MOH-shuhn)—moving or being moved

ninja (NIN-juh)—someone who is highly trained in Japanese martial arts and stealth

oxygen (OK-suh-juhn)—a colorless gas in the air that people and animals need to live

reflect (ri-FLEKT)—to bounce off an object

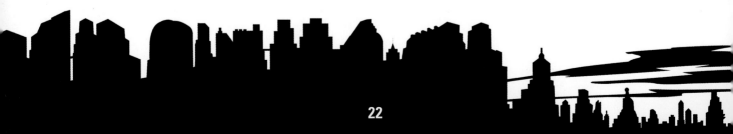

READ MORE

Gagne, Tammy. *Incredible Military Weapons*. Ready for Military Action. Minneapolis: Abdo Publishing, 2015.

Matthews, Rupert. *Weapons and Armor*. 100 Facts You Should Know. New York: Gareth Stevens Publishing, 2015.

INTERNET SITES

FactHound offers a safe, fun way to find Internet sites related to this book. All of the sites on FactHound have been researched by our staff.

Here's all you do:
Visit *www.facthound.com*
Type in this code: 9781515720386

INDEX

READ THEM ALL!

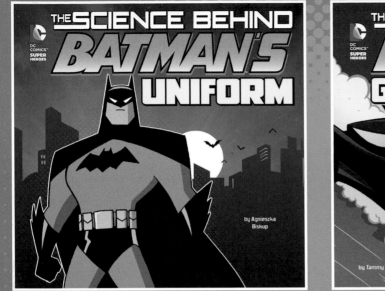

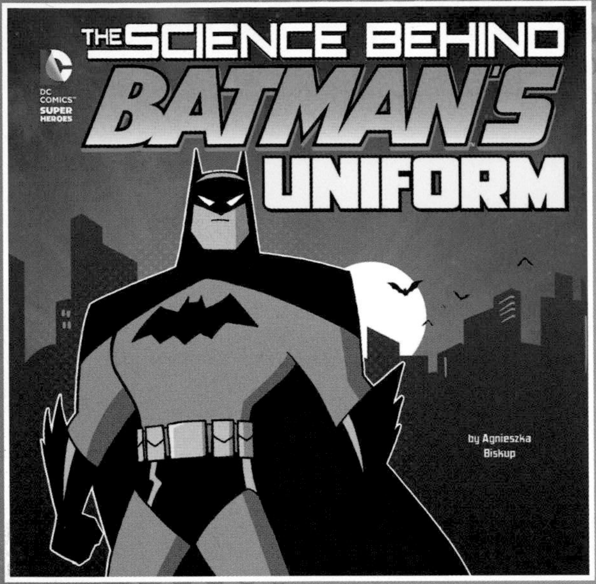
THE SCIENCE BEHIND
BATMAN'S
UNIFORM
DC COMICS SUPER HEROES
by Agnieszka Biskup

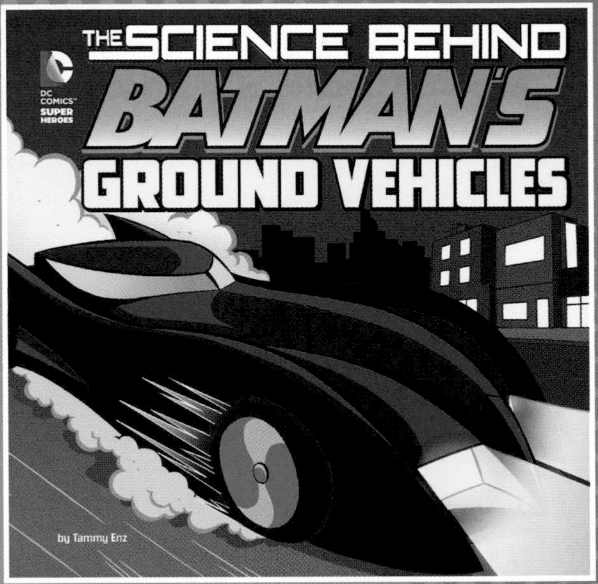
THE SCIENCE BEHIND
BATMAN'S
GROUND VEHICLES
DC COMICS SUPER HEROES
by Tammy Enz

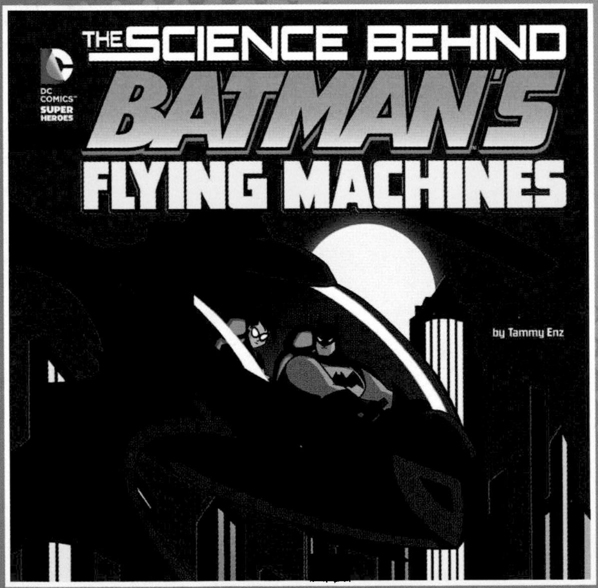
THE SCIENCE BEHIND
BATMAN'S
FLYING MACHINES
DC COMICS SUPER HEROES
by Tammy Enz

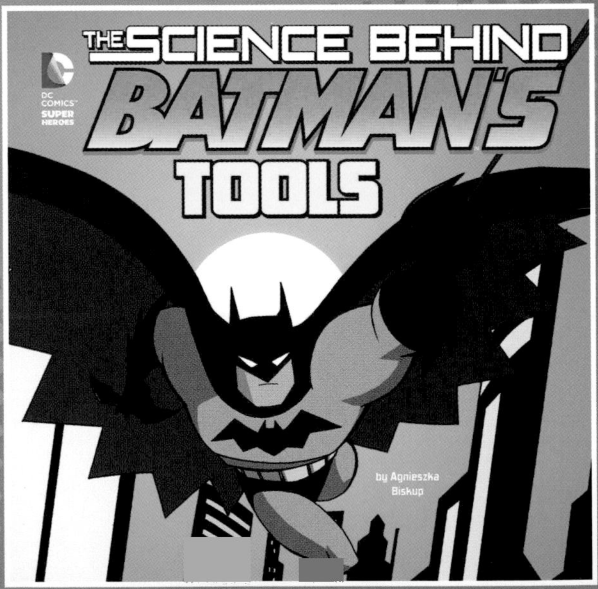
THE SCIENCE BEHIND
BATMAN'S
TOOLS
DC COMICS SUPER HEROES
by Agnieszka Biskup